Tall Ships

History Comes to Life on the Great Lakes

by Kaitlin Morrison

Adventure Publications
Cambridge, Minnesota

Acknowledgments

Many thanks to the following photographers and organizations; their photographs grace the pages of this book (see page 134 for the full photo credits): Aaron Headly, Alan Woodhead, Amy McGovern, Andrew Bone, Scott Ellis and everyone at BaySail, Bob Adams, Boris Kasimov, Christy Griffin and the staff at the Bytown Brigantine/Tall Ships Adventure, Cathy A. Smith, Dan Downing, Dave Foster, Dennis Jarvis, Erin Short at Tall Ships America, the crew of the *Fazizi*, Darren Wells and the staff of the Great Lakes Schooner Company, Hussein Abdallah, Kathy Tahtinen and the staff of *Inland Seas* Schoolship, Jeff Thoreson at *Erie Shipping News*, Jesse Davis, Joanna Poe, Kathleen Maskus/Natural Solitude, Kenneth Newhams at *Duluth Shipping News*, Lois Bravo, Lyle Vincent, Sherri at the Maritime Heritage Alliance, Martin Cathrae , Michael Greminger, Captain Andrew Sadock and Sam Perkins-Harbin of the *Red Witch*, Liz Kincheloe-Spain and the *Roseway*, Scott Colbourne, Scott Proudfoot, Shutterstock, the U.S. Navy, the U.S. Coast Guard's excellent photography staff, Will Scullin, and finally Lynn Randall and the crew of the *Windy*.

Photo credits are listed on page 136.

Edited by Brett Ortler

Cover and book design by Lora Westberg

Copyright 2016 by Kaitlin Morrison
Published by Adventure Publications
820 Cleveland Street South
Cambridge, Minnesota 55008
(800) 678-7006
www.adventurepublications.net
All rights reserved
Printed in U.S.A.
ISBN: 978-1-59193-579-7; eISBN: 978-1-59193-613-8

Dedication

This is for Jeff Greenlund, my best friend and husband.

I want to thank my entire family for supporting me throughout this journey—First, my parents, Dr. Paul Morrison, MD and Vicki Morrison for taking me to visit the Great Lakes when I was a kid and for introducing me to the wonderful world of ships.

My sister, Kelsey Morrison and my inlaws, Doug and Marla Greenlund for being constant cheerleaders. My brother-in-law, Joe Greenlund and my grandma, Barbara McDonald for challenging me to be a better person.

Of course, this book couldn't happen without the great team at Adventure Publications. I deeply appreciate my editor, Brett Ortler, for all of his hard work on this project and endless ideas. I thank God for all of the people who contributed to this book and for all of the tall ships that make this book possible.

Table of Contents

Introduction

Whether you see a tall ship breaking over the horizon, or up close at a tall ship festival, there's nothing quite like seeing a full-fledged sailing ship. These majestic vessels are often thought of as ocean-going vessels, but many tall ships ply the waters of the Great Lakes. Some have homeports on the Great Lakes, whereas others are based abroad and only visit the region occasionally, often for tall ship festivals.

Tall ship events are usually held every three years on the Great Lakes; when such events are underway, they never fail to draw tens of thousands of visitors at each port, sometimes even hundreds of thousands. Previous tall ship events were held on the Great Lakes in 2013 and 2010, and all of the vessels in this book participated in one of those events, so this book is a good introduction to the vessels that you may encounter. Of course, this doesn't mean that you'll find all of the ships in this book at a port near you; some ships only visit certain Lakes or ports, and schedules can change, equipment can break, and tall ships, perhaps more than any other kind of vessel, are subject to the vagaries of the weather. Running a tall ship is economically precarious, too, so tall ships also change owners relatively often.

The following ships represent a good cross section of the tall ships that you're likely to see on the Great Lakes. Many have homeports on the Great Lakes; those that don't are common fixtures at tall ship festivals. In addition, many of the vessels included are very accessible and open to the public for dockside tours and daysails, and many offer extended sail-training courses for youth and adults. Some can even be chartered for longer trips or events such as weddings, meetings and other private events.

So whether you see the famous *Brig Niagara* fire off its carronades or witness the majesty of tall ship after tall ship entering the harbor during a parade of sail, get out there and see a tall ship on the Great Lakes. It's an experience you'll never forget.

Parts of a Tall Ship

At its core, sailing is a relatively simple concept, but when it comes to sailing terminology, things get confusing in a hurry. Sailing, like most other fields, has its own language; thankfully, the basics aren't that hard to understand.

Tall ships are powered by sails, and float because their hull (the body of the ship) displaces water. A ship's hull is built around its keel, the ship's primary beam/support structure. If you're standing on the deck of a ship, the keel runs on a straight line from the bow (the front) of the vessel to the stern (the back of the boat). If you're standing on a ship, looking to the bow, the direction to your left is known as the port side; the direction to your right is starboard.

A tall ship is propelled largely by its sails, fabric structures that are supported by spars, wooden (or metal) supports that can be either vertical or horizontal. When spars are horizontal, they are known as yards. An angled spar that supports a sail is called a gaff. Vertical spars are known as masts. Masts can have more than one sail, and each additional sail has its own name, though listing each is beyond the scope of this book. Sails are raised/lowered by using halyards (ropes/chains) and controlled by sheets (ropes or chains that manipulate the sail).

Masts and Rigging

On a ship with three masts, the mast at the front of the vessel is called the foremast. The mast at the center of the vessel is the mainmast. If there's a third mast, it's called the mizzenmast.

The way a ship's sails and its masts are configured is known as its rigging. As you might expect, there are a hundreds of different ways to rig a ship, not to mention a number of different sails (depending on their shape/placement), so we'll only cover the basics.

Square-rigged sails are rigged perpendicular to the ship's keel. To put it in simpler terms, wind pushes on them from one side only—the back—propelling the vessel forward. Fore-and-aft rigged ships have sails that run parallel to the ship's keel, and wind can push on them from either side.

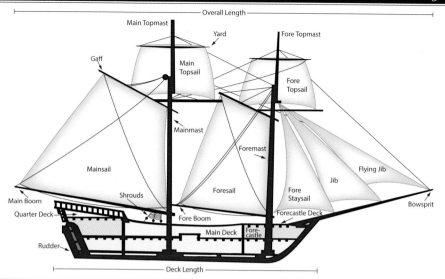

Type of Sail Plan	Description	Example
Fully rigged ship	Three or more masts, all sails square-rigged	*Bounty*
Barque	A ship with three or more masts that has all of its sails "square," or perpendicular to the keel, except on the last mast, which is rigged fore-and-aft	*Barque Europa*
Brig	Two masts, both square-rigged	*Brig Niagara*
Schooner	A ship with two or more masts; the mainmast is larger than the foremast (the front mast). Schooners are rigged with fore-and-aft sails on all lower masts. A particular type of schooner, known as the Great Lakes Schooner, became very popular as a cargo carrier on the Great Lakes in the nineteenth century and the early twentieth century.	*S/V Denis Sullivan*
Gaff-rigged topsail schooner	A ship with two more masts rigged with fore-and-aft sails, which are controlled by a diagonal wooden spar called a gaff; this type of schooner can also feature a topsail	*Unicorn*
Baltimore clipper	A ship with a very streamlined hull, and taller-than-usual masts; built for speed, Baltimore clippers had a variety of sail plans	*Pride of Baltimore II*
Sloop	A ship with one mast bearing a fore-and-aft mainsail, and a jib, a triangular sail at the front of the vessel for added control	*Fazisi*
Square topsail sloop	A sloop that also has a square-rigged topsail	*Friends Good Will*
Brigantine	A ship with two masts that has the foremast square-rigged, and the mainmast fore-and-aft rigged, with a square-rigged topsail above that	*Fair Jeanne*
Windjammer	A sailing ship with multiple masts (often three to five) and square-rigged sails, but built with a steel hull; these were among the last cargo vessels powered by sail	*Roseway*

Tall Ship Homeports on the Great Lakes

Minnesota
LAKE SUPERIOR
Zeeto
Duluth, MN
Coaster II
Marquette, MI
Wisconsin
Inland Seas
Suttons Bay, MI
Madeline
Traverse City, MI
LAKE MICHIGAN
Michigan
S/V Denis Sullivan
Milwaukee, WI
Friends Good Will
South Haven, MI
Iowa
Empire Sandy/Fazisi
/Red Witch/Windy
Chicago, IL
Illinois
Indiana

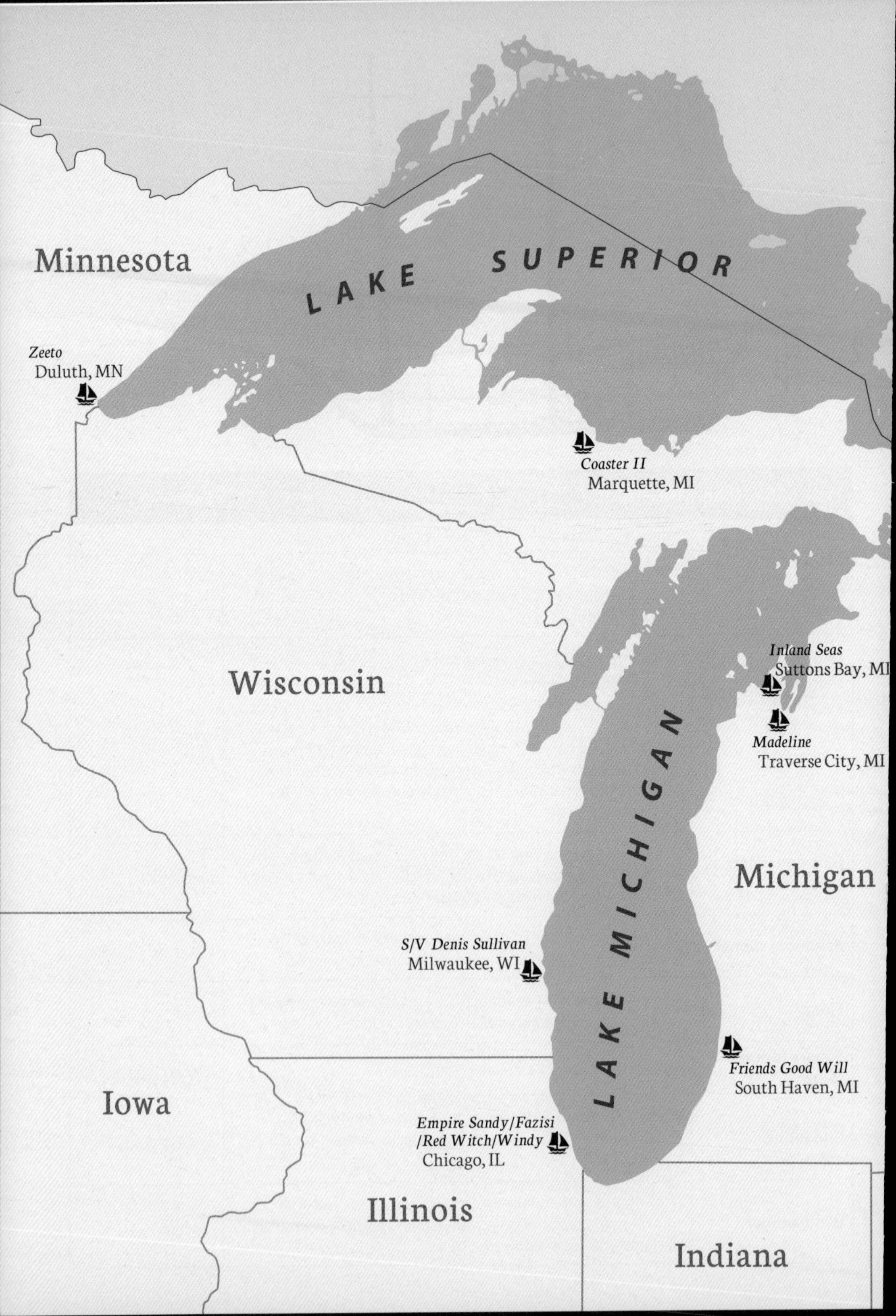

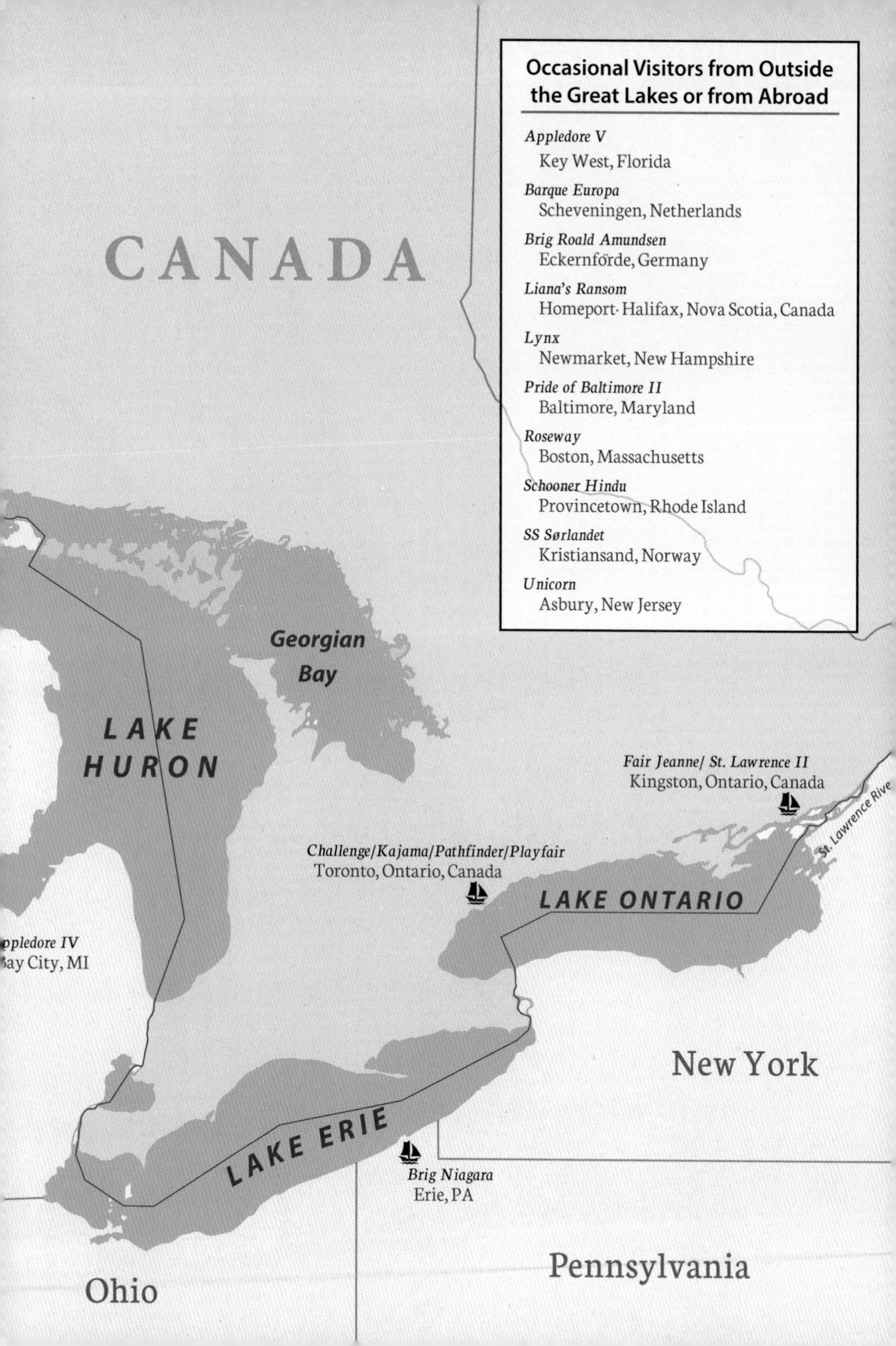

Occasional Visitors from Outside the Great Lakes or from Abroad
Appledore V
Key West, Florida
Barque Europa
Scheveningen, Netherlands
Brig Roald Amundsen
Eckernförde, Germany
Liana's Ransom
Homeport· Halifax, Nova Scotia, Canada
Lynx
Newmarket, New Hampshire
Pride of Baltimore II
Baltimore, Maryland
Roseway
Boston, Massachusetts
Schooner Hindu
Provincetown, Rhode Island
SS Sørlandet
Kristiansand, Norway
Unicorn
Asbury, New Jersey
CANADA
Georgian Bay
LAKE HURON
Fair Jeanne/ St. Lawrence II
Kingston, Ontario, Canada
St. Lawrence Rive
Challenge/Kajama/Pathfinder/Playfair
Toronto, Ontario, Canada
LAKE ONTARIO
ppledore IV
ay City, MI
New York
LAKE ERIE
Brig Niagara
Erie, PA
Pennsylvania
Ohio

APPLEDORE V

Appledore V: Sea Stories

The *Appledore V* is one in the series of *Appledore* tall ships commissioned by Herb and Doris Smith for their globe-trotting adventures. With a steel hull and modern accommodations, the *Appledore V* is designed for ocean-faring voyages and can handle treacherous waters, as the Smiths proved when they sailed it to locations all around the world. The first ship in the *Appledore* series, the *Appledore I*, was built by the Smiths (with some help) around Herbert Smith's busy schedule as a cinematographer at Disney. Once completed, the Smith family took their ships to sea, and they haven't stopped since. Along the way, they've built a whole series of vessels and have traveled the world over, from the Caribbean to Pitcairn Island (famous for being the refuge of the *Bounty* mutineers).

The fifth *Appledore* vessel, the *Appledore V* sailed under a different name after the Smiths sold her to the Traverse Tall Ship Company where she was renamed the *Westwind*. There, she served as a sailing bed-and-breakfast, and in the process the *Westwind* made fewer seafaring voyages and began spending more time on the Great Lakes. She was then purchased by BaySail, a nonprofit educational organization, and today both the *Appledore V* and the *Appledore IV* are owned by the group. The *Appledore V* offers tours near Key West, Florida, and both ships are floating classrooms for environmental and sailing education programs. During the summer, the *Appledore V* spends much of her time in the Great Lakes visiting locations such as Mackinac Island and the North Channel of Lake Huron and is crewed largely by sailing students. Whenever she participates in tall ship festivals, the *Appledore V* continues to dazzle and impress passengers and onlookers alike.

8

Ship Details

Year Built: 1992 • **Type of Ship:** Two-masted schooner • **Country Built:** USA • **Homeport:** Key West, Florida • **Overall length:** 65 feet • **Beam (width at widest point):** 14 feet • **Maximum Mast Height:** 63 feet • **Armament:** None • **Crew:** 3

Construction

The *Appledore V* has a steel hull, like her sister ship, the *Appledore IV*. Famed shipbuilder Bud McIntosh designed the *Appledore V,* and she was constructed by Treworgy Yachts. She can accommodate as many as 32 passengers and crew, with sleeping quarters for 12. Her 90-horsepower diesel engine helps her sail through difficult waterways and unfriendly weather better than with wind power alone.

Barque Europa

Barque Europa: Sea Stories

This beautiful ship was constructed in Germany in 1911 as a lightship for the State of Hamburg; it was rebuilt as a barque in 1994. As a lightship, she was known by the name *Senator Brockes*, and her original purpose was to serve as a navigational beacon where lighthouses were impractical. In her long career, she was active along the Elbe River.

After her career as a lightship ended in the 1980s, she was retired and later sold and brought to Holland, where she was renamed the *Barque Europa*. This ship was extensively rebuilt and transformed into a type of tall ship known as a barque (see page 7). She was then dedicated as a training platform for the next generation of tall ship sailors while doubling as a unique vacation destination for travelers from around the world. Today, she serves as a floating sailing school and a charter ship, and belongs to the Bark Europa Company. The *Barque Europa* now happily sails to Antarctica, Cape Horn and other enchanting destinations. She also visits the Great Lakes on occasion and sometimes races against other tall ships, usually faring well against larger vessels.

Barque Europa's hull is decorated with figures from the Greek mythological tale of Europa. These figures replace older decorations that originally adorned the ship when she was reconstructed. The newest figures were made by Lynx Guimand and added to the *Barque Europa's* hull in 2010 after the older decorations were damaged by an iceberg during a trip to Antarctica.

Year Built: 1911 (original build); 1986–1994 (restoration) • **Type of Ship:** Three-masted barque • **Country Built:** Germany • **Homeport:** Scheveningen, Netherlands • **Overall length:** 183 feet • **Beam (width at widest point):** 24 feet • **Maximum Mast Height:** 108 feet • **Armament:** None • **Original Crew:** 3–7 (typical lightship crew) • **Present Crew:** 11–16 (with up to 48 crew in training)

——————— *Construction* ———————

This ship was originally constructed for use in Germany as a lightship and was reconstructed as a three-masted barque schooner after she was retired from German Federal Coast Guard service. She was constructed in Hamburg, Germany, on the Stülcken Wharf. Manned lightships were gradually replaced by buoys, unmanned vessels and lighthouses, and most lightships were retired by the 1980s. The *Europa's* rebuild was extensive. She was rerigged, thoroughly updated inside and out and now uses as many as 30 sails. She has two 365-horsepower engines and a hardened steel hull to contend with Antarctic ice, as well as six watertight compartments that provide stability and help protect the ship.

BOUNTY

GREENPORT
NEW YORK

Bounty: Sea Stories

Built in 1960 for the MGM film *Mutiny on the Bounty*, the *Bounty* was an accurate, albeit larger, replica of the original *HMS Bounty*, which was constructed in 1784 by the Royal Navy of Great Britain. Constructed using traditional methods and reproduced from the blueprints of the original ship, the vessel had very few modifications other than the increased size, which was necessary to support camera equipment. After the film was completed, MGM's owner, Ted Turner, donated the ship to the city of Fall River, Massachusetts, where it was hoped that the *Bounty* would help drive tourism. Unfortunately, the repairs that *Bounty* needed proved to be too expensive, and the ship was resold to the HMS Bounty Foundation, based out of New York. Her new owner repaired and renovated the ship and offered sailing excursions, sail training, as well as public tours.

Unfortunately the *Bounty's* days were numbered. Always taking on water even in the best of conditions, she was in almost constant need of repair. Nonetheless, her owner and crew continued to participate in some tall ship festivals and other events. The *Bounty* was booked to participate in an event in October of 2012. The event was in St. Petersburg, Florida, and her captain made the fateful decision to set sail from Connecticut despite the forecast approach of Superstorm Sandy. The *Bounty's* captain, Robin Walbridge, directed the ship to avoid the hurricane by heading east at first; he then crossed west, in front the storm, in the hopes of "squeaking by" the storm. This ended in disaster, as the *Bounty* sank off the coast of Cape Hatteras, North Carolina. The U.S. Coast Guard rescued 14 of the people aboard, but one crew member's body was recovered in the water, and the captain was never found.

Year Built: 1960 • **Type of Ship:** Three-masted, full-rigged ship • **Country Built:** Canada • **Homeport:** Greenport, New York • **Overall length:** 180 feet • **Beam (width at widest point):** 32 feet • **Maximum Mast Height:** 111 feet • **Original Armament:** Four 4-pound guns • **Restoration Armament:** None • **Original Crew:** 44 • **Crew (when lost):** 16

Construction

The *Bounty* is a replica of the original *HMS Bounty*, which was constructed in 1784 in Great Britain. The replica ship was longer than the original, with the replica being 118 feet long on the deck. The original was only 91 feet long. This larger size provided additional space for cameras and film crews aboard the *Bounty*. The replica had two 375-horsepower diesel engines and other modern equipment, but like the original, the *Bounty* had a wood hull that was subject to constant wear-and-tear and prone to leaking.

Brig Niagara

Brig Roald Amundsen: Sea Stories

Named after the first explorer to reach the South Pole, the *Brig Roald Amundsen* is based out of her homeport of Eckernförde, Germany, but she travels to locales near and far. No matter where she goes, the goals are the same: she presents new sailors with the opportunity to learn how navigate and maintain a tall ship. Her owners strongly believe in sailing and the life lessons taught by the sea.

The *Brig Roald Amundsen* was originally known as the *Vilm*. Originally designed for deep-sea fishing, she soon became a supply ship and a tanker for the East German National People's Army. With the fall of the Berlin Wall, she was no longer needed. In 1992, she was restored and put to use as a training ship for sailors. Her new life began in 1993, with Immo von Schnurbein as the first captain. A German nonprofit organization, *LebenLernen auf Segelschiffen* (Living and Learning from Sailing Ships) owns and operates the *Brig Roald Amundsen*. Today, the ship sails year-round, and nearly 500 new tall ship sailors train aboard her each year. Her dedicated volunteer crew members also cumulatively contribute thousands of hours while maintaining and sailing the vessel year-round. Each volunteer is usually aboard for a two- or three-week voyage.

The *Amundsen's* destinations vary by season. In the summer, she frequents ports on the Baltic Sea, and her winter adventures take her to the Canary Islands and locations farther south. She also enters tall ship races across the globe, occasionally visiting the Great Lakes area for its races and festivals.

Year Built: 1952 (original), restored and converted to a brig in 1992 • **Type of Ship:** Brig • **Country Built:** Germany • **Homeport:** Eckernförde, Germany • **Overall length:** 164 feet • **Beam (width at widest point):** 23 feet • **Maximum Mast Height:** 111 feet • **Armament:** None • **Original Crew:** Unknown, but up to 79 (maximum capacity) • **Present Crew:** 17 crew and 31 trainees

Construction

Originally, a supply ship and a tanker for the East German Army, she was converted to a tall ship in 1992. This included a rerigging with a new total of 18 sails. She has modern safety and navigational equipment, including a 300-horsepower diesel engine, generators and a GPS. Two other ships, the *Fridtjof Nansen* and the *Umberto Nobile*, were also rerigged and renovated for sail training along with the *Roald Amundsen*. They were also named after polar explorers and were all rebuilt at the Fridtjof Nansen Wharf in Wolgast, Germany.

Challenge: Sea Stories

The *Challenge* is a replica schooner made in honor of the 1852 ship of the same name. The original *Challenge* typically transported freight, and spent her career sailing Lake Michigan. Nicknamed the "Belle of Lake Michigan," she was famous for being the very first clipper constructed on the Great Lakes, and her new design soon became the standard on the Great Lakes, thanks to her speed and reliability. Over the coming decades, thousands of these "Michigan schooners" would ply the lakes. The original *Challenge* carried wood and other freight on the Great Lakes and served for more than half a century; she was purposely scuttled in 1910 after she was no longer needed.

Years of exposure to the elements finally caused her keel to wash up on the Lake Michigan shore. Kohler-Andrae State Park's nature center now displays what remains of the proud schooner.

The present-day *Challenge* was built in 1980 and transported passengers during her early years. Voyages within the Great Lakes were common, and she also occasionally ventured to the Virgin Islands. Today, the ship is owned by Tall Ship Cruises Toronto, where she hosts visitors for daysails trips as well as sightseeing trips. These cruises are open to the public and allow travelers to enjoy the scenery of the Great Lakes and the Toronto Harbor.

Ship Details

Year Built: 1980 (original 1852) • **Type of Ship:** Three-masted schooner • **Country Built:** Canada • **Homeport:** Toronto, Ontario, Canada • **Overall length:** 96 feet • **Beam (width at widest point):** 16 feet • **Maximum Mast Height:** 90 feet • **Armament:** None • **Crew:** Varies

Construction

Challenge was constructed at Port Stanley, Ontario, by the Kanter Yacht Company in 1980 based on the 1852 ship, built in Cleveland, Ohio. Fully modernized, she now can host up to 72 guests, and even boasts a licensed bar and DJ services.

Empire Sandy: Sea Stories

Built in 1943 in Great Britain, the *Empire Sandy* was constructed as a deep-sea tug for service in World War II. One of the United Kingdom's famous class of "Empire Ships" (akin to the Liberty Ships built in the U.S.), the *Empire Sandy's* six wartime missions took her to Iceland, Sri Lanka, France, Sierra Leone and other locations around the world as well as within the United Kingdom. Her logbooks from these voyages record the tales of her adventures. For all but one of her voyages, the *Empire Sandy* traveled with other ships, which provided her some protection against German U-boats. Still, given how many ships were sunk during the Battle of the Atlantic, her crossings were risky, and several crew desertions were recorded in her logbooks. During her first voyage, *Empire Sandy's* cook deserted ship and never returned, presumably leaving the rest of the crew with lackluster meals as a result of his absence. After the war, *Empire Sandy* was used to transport salvage materials and would soon undergo several name changes. She was renamed the *Ashford* in 1948 and *Chris M.* in 1952 before finally being rechristened as *Empire Sandy* in 1979. Through these long working years, she served a number of different owners, including the Great Lakes Paper Company, Gravel and Lake Services and finally Stratheame Terminals. It was the Great Lakes Paper Company that initially brought her to Canada, which has been her home ever since. In 1982, the ship was converted into a three-masted schooner. She now serves as a charter ship for special events and sightseeing trips. She can accommodate as many as 180 daysail passengers comfortably below deck and up to 275 daytime passengers total. She now explores the Great Lakes and regularly participates in tall ship events.

Year Built: 1943 • **Type of Ship:** Three-masted schooner • **Country Built:** UK • **Homeport:** Toronto, Ontario, Canada • **Overall length:** 203 feet • **Beam (width at widest point):** 30 feet • **Maximum Mast Height:** 116 feet • **Original Armament:** 2 Hotchkiss anti-aircraft guns • **Armament Today:** None • **Original Crew:** 19 • **Present Crew:** 25 (maximum)

Construction

The *Empire Sandy* was converted from a deep-sea tugboat to a traditional-style schooner with three masts in 1982. As a tugboat, she was designed with accommodations for extended voyages with sleeping quarters. Below deck, she now accommodates seating for up to 180 event guests but no longer can accommodate overnight passengers. Despite the redesign, she retains her original durable steel hull, and she's also been outfitted with a modern diesel engine for additional propulsion.

Fair Jeanne

Fair Jeanne: Sea Stories

The *Fair Jeanne* was built in 1982 as a personal yacht for Captain Thomas G. Fuller, a renowned former officer in Canada's navy during World War II. During his wartime service, Fuller was known as the "Pirate of the Adriatic" for his wildly successful and audacious raids on Axis shipping off the coast of what was then Yugoslavia. He and his men operated the fast, but poorly armored, Motor Torpedo Boats, which enabled him to capture many enemy cargo vessels. He gave the tons of supplies that he salvaged to opponents of the Axis forces. On occasion, he even took enemy prisoners. In one instance, he rescued a number of German submariners whose vessel sunk; one of them was a cook, and Fuller soon hired him to serve as his own vessel's cook!

The *Fair Jeanne* began as Fuller's personal yacht, and he sailed around the world aboard the vessel with his wife, stopping in various locations in Europe and the Caribbean. After his death in 1994, the ship eventually became a sail-training ship for Bytown Brigantine Academy, an organization founded by Simon Fuller, one of Fuller's sons.

Today, Bytown Brigantine teaches young sailing students the basics of tall ship sailing. *Fair Jeanne* provides sailing adventures for teens and adults, while her sister ship *Black Jack* offers younger teens the opportunity to learn sailing and participate in an island camp. *Fair Jeanne* also occasionally participates in public tall ship events on the Great Lakes.

Ship Details

Year Built: 1982 • **Type of Ship:** Brigantine • **Country Built:** Canada • **Homeport:** Kingston, Ontario, Canada • **Overall length:** 110 feet • **Beam (width at widest point):** 24 feet • **Maximum Mast Height:** 80 feet • **Armament:** None • **Crew:** 6

Construction

Between 1979 and 1982, Captain Fuller built the *Fair Jeanne* in his backyard. Captain Fuller named her in honor of his wife, Jeanne. The ship was repaired after a collision in 2013, when another ship ran into her one early morning after she had been anchored for the night.

Fazisi

L'AMOUR
CRISSCUT®

ISTOPHER DESIGNS
CRISSCUT®
· NEW YORK ·

Fazisi: Sea Stories

Constructed in the Georgian Soviet Socialist Republic, *Fazisi* was completed in 1989 and was intended to represent the Soviet Union in the grueling Whitbread Round the World Race (today known as the Volvo Ocean Race). The *Fazisi* was named after the legendary Phasis River—now known as the Rioni—where Jason and the Argonauts reputedly discovered the famous Golden Fleece. Like the famous story that inspired its name, the boat's very participation in the Whitbread Race was something of an epic undertaking in itself. To begin with, the *Fazisi's* initial construction and racing budget were just a fraction of that of the competition, and that was before she lost her primary sponsor, Pepsico. This calamity was followed by her co-captain's tragic suicide, no doubt due to the pressure of the overall situation. Somewhat amazingly, her crew persevered, essentially fundraising along the way. Volunteers outside of the Soviet Union raised additional support, helping repay some of boat's debts. Throughout the race, the crew exhibited memorable resourcefulness and not only finished the race but somehow held their own, finishing 11th out of 21 boats.

Members of the Joseph Conrad Yacht Club in Chicago bought *Fazisi* in 1999 and the ship was relocated to the United States. She was entered in races in the Great Lakes, in 2000 and 2001. Later, *Fazisi* was donated to the Polish Yachting Association of North America. Recently refurbished, the *Fazisi* now welcomes sailing students aboard, all while visiting locations in Bermuda, Cuba, and other ports. *Fazisi* has won numerous awards and she continues to sail in the Great Lakes while undertaking voyages worldwide.

Year Built: 1989 • **Type of Ship:** Sloop • **Country Built:** Soviet Union • **Homeport:** Chicago, Illinois; Brooklyn, New York • **Overall length:** 83 feet • **Beam (width at widest point):** 19 feet • **Maximum Mast Height:** 100 feet • **Armament:** None • **Crew:** Up to 14

—————— *Construction* ——————

Designed by Vlad Murnikow, *Fazisi* was the only ship that represented the Soviet Union in a Whitbread Round the World Race. She has an aluminum hull, simple accommodations for her crew, and modern communication and navigational equipment. Above all, *Fazisi* was designed for speed, so she carries a minimum of creature comforts. The boat looks somewhat like a shark from underneath, with shark-like fins and part of a tail when viewed from underwater. When it comes to performance, the unique design has paid off; during the Whitbread Race, she covered an amazing 386 nautical miles in 24 hours, good for an astonishing 18 mile-per-hour clip.

Friends Good Will: Sea Stories

Friends Good Will is a replica of the famous warship of the same name that served in the War of 1812. The original ship was constructed in 1810 and participated in the Battle of Lake Erie. She was built as a merchant ship, and was transporting fresh supplies to Fort Dearborn when she was captured by the British. She was renamed *Little Belt* and armed for warfare. During the famous battle of October 1813, she was captured by Oliver Hazard Perry and again served the United States, transporting American soldiers across Lake Erie, supporting the unsuccessful American invasion of Southern Ontario. Unfortunately, the *Friends Good Will* was beached in a storm in 1813, and the British set her ablaze at the beginning of 1814.

In honor of the original ship, a replica of the *Friends Good Will* was constructed in 2004. Operated by the Michigan Maritime Museum, the new ship sails as a memorial to the proud original, and it offers a wide variety of sailing excursions, from daysails and sunset sails to kid-friendly "pirate chaser" excursions. On occasion, the crew even dresses in period costumes. If you're interested in a more private outing, the ship can also be chartered for events and weddings.

Ship Details

Year Built: 1810 (original); replica built in 2004 • **Type of Ship:** Square topsail sloop • **Country Built:** USA • **Homeport:** South Haven, Michigan • **Overall length:** 101 feet • **Beam (width at widest point):** 16 feet • **Maximum Mast Height:** 80 feet • **Original Armament:** One 9-pound gun and two 6-pounders • **Armament Today:** One 6-pound gun • **Original Crew:** 13 • **Present Crew:** 13

Construction

The *Friends Good Will* replica is not an exact copy of the original ship. Traditional construction methods were not used when producing the vessel; utilizing modern methods helps the ship accommodate passengers and remain easier to maintain. Nevertheless, the ship was crafted to closely resemble a traditionally built vessel. Wood laminate construction was chosen, allowing portions of the ship to be built from multiple pieces of wood, instead of requiring each piece to be carved from a single tree. All rigging and sails are created from modern materials, but they are designed to appear authentic to the nineteenth century.

Kajama: Sea Stories

The *Kajama* was first known as the *Wilfred* and was constructed as a three-masted schooner in 1930 at a German shipyard. *Wilfred* belonged to Captain Wilhelm Wilckens and sailed out of Hamburg as a cargo ship between 1930 and 1960, until the ship was sold to a Dane, Captain Karl Asmussen. He christened the ship *Kajama*, and the name was an amalgamation of letters from his family members' names. He drew the letters "K" and "A" from his son Kaywe; "J" and "A" from his son Jan; the letters "M" and "A" for his wife, Maria. The ship's name is pronounced "Kye-YAH-ma."

In the 1970s *Kajama* was rebuilt and converted to a solely engine-powered vessel. Captain Karl Asmussen continued to man her until 1998, when he died at the helm of the ship due to a heart attack. The next year, *Kajama* was sold to Great Lakes Schooner Company of Toronto. The company began sailing *Kajama* as a charter ship, and her new owners transformed her back into a schooner, completing all the restoration work in under a year. She now takes passengers on short adventure excursions, daytime cruises and private charters. She's equipped with a full kitchen, a licensed bar, DJ services (upon request) and can host up to 225 guests.

Her sister ship, *Challenge*, also sails with the Great Lakes Schooner Company, and both ships provide visitors with the opportunity to sail the Great Lakes aboard authentic schooners.

Year Built: 1930 • **Type of Ship:** Schooner • **Country Built:** Germany • **Homeport:** Toronto, Ontario, Canada • **Overall length:** 164 feet • **Beam (width at widest point):** 23 feet • **Maximum Mast Height:** 98 feet • **Armament:** A small cannon is fired on every cruise • **Crew:** Varies

———— *Construction* ————

Kajama was built as a cargo vessel, and her design was mass-produced as she was a cheap ship to run and could be helmed by a small crew. Despite her age, she is a sturdy vessel; she ran aground on a sandbar in the 1990s, but the accident resulted in only minor damage.

Liana's Ransom: Sea Stories

Styled after the pirate ships of old, *Liana's Ransom's* crew members dress in pirate costumes and transport passengers on sightseeing adventures. Constructed in 1998, the ship has an eighteenth- or nineteenth-century feel. Her crew teaches passengers about sailing the ship, firing the cannons and hoisting sails during each pirate-themed trip.

Even though she's a faux pirate ship, *Liana's Ransom* has experienced some very real danger. In December of 2014, the ship lost her mainmast, but thankfully no one was hurt. In March 2015, the ship lost power in the throes of a gale that produced 10-foot waves. She also lost her mainmast in the incident. The U.S. Coast Guard soon arrived on scene and attempted to tow the disabled ship back, but the tow line broke, and the weather worsened, causing the crew to abandon ship for the safety of the nearby Coast Guard vessels. Happily, all aboard were rescued, and *Liana's Ransom* survived the storm (an emergency satellite beacon had been placed aboard her to track her position), and she has since been repaired and continues to embark upon voyages today.

Liana's Ransom spends significant time sailing in such far-flung locations as the Caribbean, but she also makes appearances in the Great Lakes and participates in tall ship events. Wherever she goes, the appearance of a pirate ship on the horizon dazzles onlookers and reminds her fans of a wild, fascinating time when swashbucklers ruled the world's oceans.

Ship Details

Year Built: 1998–2002 • **Type of Ship:** Gaff-rigged topsail schooner • **Country Built:** USA • **Homeport:** Halifax, Nova Scotia, Canada • **Overall length:** 85 feet • **Beam (width at widest point):** 21 feet • **Maximum Mast Height:** 75 feet • **Armament:** Four 24-pound black powder cannons • **Crew:** 3–5

Construction

Liana's Ransom was rebuilt as a gaff-rigged schooner in 2006 and 2007. Originally, she was constructed as a staysail schooner. Rather than taking inspiration from Great Lakes schooners, this pirate ship look-alike was constructed based on typical Gulf of Mexico schooners from the 1700s and 1800s. She was also outfitted with replica cannons that are used during demonstrations on voyages.

Madeline: Sea Stories

The schooner *Madeline* is a 1980s replica of a beautiful 1845 freight vessel of the same name. Operated by the Maritime Heritage Alliance, the new *Madeline* serves her community as an educational ship and her crew teaches visitors about the long maritime history of the Great Lakes and the importance of the thousands of schooners that once plied the Great Lakes in the service of industry.

Interestingly enough, the original *Madeline* also played an educational role. In fact, this ship served as one of the first schools in the area. Her captain and crew decided they wanted to further their education during the winter of 1851 and 1852. For one season, they brought the *Madeline* to Bowers Harbor in Traverse City and hired a local teacher, making the *Madeline* a floating school. While afternoons were spent maintaining the ship, doing chores and having fun, mornings were set aside for serious study of reading, writing and arithmetic. The group soon became well-educated enough to pursue their career goals and set off to continue running their previous enterprise on the *Madeline*. In the end, the men all stayed in the Great Lakes region and led successful careers, thanks, in part, to their newfound education.

Construction of the new *Madeline* began in 1985 and ended in 1990. Volunteers from the Maritime Heritage Alliance donated 40,000 work hours to the project, and the ship soon began serving as an educational museum. Maintenance care for *Madeline* and ongoing operations are financed by donations. Much of this support comes from local individuals and groups interested in preserving maritime history in the Great Lakes region.

Year Built: 1845 (original); current reconstruction built from 1985-1990 • **Type of Ship**: Schooner • **Country Built**: USA • **Homeport**: Traverse City, Michigan • **Overall length**: 92 feet • **Beam (width at widest point)**: 16 feet • **Maximum Mast Height**: 71 feet • **Armament**: None • **Original Crew**: 5 • **Present Crew**: 5-6

———— *Construction* ————

The replica *Madeline* is somewhat bigger than the original, with a deck length of 56 feet compared with her predecessor's deck length of 52. At 92 feet overall, the new *Madeline* is a smaller schooner than many of the famous nineteenth-century schooners, some of which were several hundred feet long. Constructing the new *Madeline* required a large number of volunteers; 165 people contributed volunteer hours to her construction.

Playfair: Sea Stories

Built specifically for sail training, *Playfair* serves as a floating classroom along with her sister ship, *Pathfinder*. When the Toronto Brigantine organization wanted to expand their successful sail-training program for young people, they needed another ship. Applications for the nonprofit's programs greatly exceeded capacity, and the organization's board of directors decided to ask *Pathfinder's* designer, Francis Maclachlan, to design another ship. Using a similar design to the *Pathfinder* and *St. Lawrence II*, Maclachlan made a few modifications to *Playfair's* blueprints and construction of the ship began. In 1973, *Playfair* was built and was officially christened by Queen Elizabeth II. In fact, this made *Playfair* the very first Canadian ship to be named by a reigning monarch.

Playfair teaches around 300 tall ship students every year, and more than 20,000 students have learned tall ship skills aboard *Playfair* or *Pathfinder*. *Playfair* sails over 4,000 miles per year, and during its youth programs, the captain of the ship is the only adult aboard. The other officers are all young people who have completed a special training program. The young crew, usually aged 13 to 18, serve on the ship and live and work aboard her during a short one- to two-week voyage to different Great Lakes ports. While at sea, the crew is divided into watches, with each watch operating within the ship's chain of command. Different groups control the ship during each two- to four-hour watch, all under the guidance of the *Playfair's* captain. Typically, *Playfair* sails for two or three days between ports and offers "shore leave" to crew members while the ship is at port.

Year Built: 1973 • **Type of Ship:** Brigantine • **Country Built:** Canada • **Homeport:** Toronto, Ontario, Canada • **Overall length:** 72 feet • **Beam (width at widest point):** 15 feet • **Maximum Mast Height:** 57 feet • **Armament:** None • **Crew:** 28 (with 18 trainees)

—————— *Construction* ——————

Playfair is very similar in design and construction to her sister ships, *St. Lawrence II* and *Pathfinder*. This ship was designed after the Toronto Brigantine program had been operating *Pathfinder* for a decade. *Playfair* shares the same dimensions as her sister ship, the *Pathfinder*.

Red Witch: Sea Stories

This beautiful ship's name was inspired by Garland Roark's *Wake of the Red Witch*, a book that was adapted for film in 1948. With a deep red hull and traditional sails, this small schooner makes quite an impression on onlookers as she sails the Great Lakes as a charter and tour ship. Constructed in 1986, she was crafted specifically to transport passengers on daysails. She has enjoyed a successful charter ship career since the year she was built. Her crew enjoys getting adventurous passengers involved in hoisting sails and other aspects of sailing during her short voyages exploring the Chicago shoreline. When she is not providing tours of the Great Lakes, the vessel hosts camps for young people and group activities for tall ship fans of all ages.

Her design is reminiscent of nineteenth-century schooners, a class of ships that contributed significantly to the industry and commerce of the Great Lakes region during the 1800s. While schooners eventually began to fall out of favor for commercial use, schooners continue to enjoy tremendous popularity as charter vessels. Many ships similar to *Red Witch* provide armchair sailors with tours of the Great Lakes, but the *Red Witch* stands out as a cruise ship. With a hull made from red mahogany imported from Honduras and a stunning traditional design, *Red Witch* brings the spirit of the high seas to the Great Lakes region.

Year Built: 1986 • **Type of Ship:** Schooner • **Country Built:** USA • **Homeport:** Chicago, Illinois • **Overall length:** 77 feet • **Beam (width at widest point):** 18 feet • **Maximum Mast Height:** 73 feet • **Armament:** None • **Crew:** Varies

──────── *Construction* ────────

Designed by John Alden, *Red Witch*'s hull consists of Honduran mahogany over oak, and the ship can accommodate as many as 49 daysail passengers. With an overall length of 77 feet, she is a relatively small schooner and similar to many of the traditional schooners once found on the Great Lakes in the nineteenth century.

S/V Dennis Sullivan: Sea Stories

S/V Denis Sullivan is a replica of one of the most important types of ship ever to sail the Great Lakes—the Great Lakes schooner. These ships were a common sight in the nineteenth century and served as the backbone of water transport on the Great Lakes. Commercial activity relied heavily on these ships and their popularity gave such schooners a significant place in regional history. Constructed with the goal of recapturing this history, *S/V Denis Sullivan* is the result of more than 900,000 volunteer hours and the relentless efforts of Milwaukee residents. When she sails locally and on voyages around the world, she represents Milwaukee and serves as an emissary on behalf of the Great Lakes and the environment.

As an educational ship, the *S/V Denis Sullivan* provides training programs about environmental science, and she also conducts field research. She offers a variety of sail-training opportunities and science education programs for K-12 students, as well as to outside clubs and groups. Students and teachers aboard the *Sullivan* have traveled as far abroad as Belize, the Caribbean and other distant locations. She has even hosted a vocational program onboard for students to learn tall ship skills.

Dubbed the official flagship of Wisconsin, *S/V Denis Sullivan* travels as a representative of both the state and environmental and ecological issues. She has even received official recognition by the United Nations for her efforts. Today, the *Sullivan* is a common sight at tall ship festivals and events.

Year Built: 1994–2000 • **Type of Ship:** Three-masted Great Lakes schooner • **Country Built:** USA • **Homeport:** Milwaukee, Wisconsin • **Overall length:** 137 feet • **Beam (width at widest point):** 23 feet • **Maximum Mast Height:** 95 feet • **Armament:** None • **Crew:** 10

———— *Construction* ————

S/V Denis Sullivan was constructed thanks to donations and volunteers, and this process took time. She was built between 1994 and 2000, with the initial project beginning in 1991. She was designed by Timothy Graul, from Marine Design of Sturgeon Bay, Wisconsin. Her design was based in part on the *Moonlight*, a nineteenth-century schooner sailed by Captain Denis Sullivan and remembered as the "Queen of the Lakes" for her speed and reputation. She was built with many traditional materials, such as white oak, Douglas fir and cloth sails. Like most modern tall ships, she also has modern equipment such as diesel engines and a generator, enabling her to accommodate 21 overnight participants or 45 total sailors during daytime voyages.

Schooner Hindu: Sea Stories

Built in 1925, this ship was originally known as the *Princess Pat* and was named after the British Princess Patricia of Connaught. The *Princess Pat* was initially a personal yacht and changed owners and names several times. She was known as the *Saispas* and the *Anna Lee Ames* before she was dubbed the *Schooner Hindu* after being purchased by William J. Parker in the late 1930s. Soon thereafter she sailed to India in 1938, a country she visited on several occasions while delivering spices to the U.S.

During World War II, the U.S. Coast Guard used *Schooner Hindu* to watch for German submarines and other threats on the East Coast. Although *Schooner Hindu* is fairly small when compared with many other tall ships, she was still formidable during her wartime service, as she was armed with a machine gun and depth charges. Her wooden construction also gave her a low radar cross section, making her an almost ideal patrol ship.

After the war, *Schooner Hindu* served as a charter ship in Provincetown, Massachusetts, where she took passengers on whale-watching trips for the next several decades before the ship began to fall apart due to neglect. Her restoration began in 2006 and was led by Keven "Foggy" Foley, who served as part of the *Schooner Hindu's* crew when he was just 12 years old. Much of the ship was rebuilt with new materials. Foley then used her as a charter ship, with *Schooner Hindu* spending her summers in Provincetown and wintering in Key West just as she does today. Unfortunately, the ship eventually became bank-owned and suffered more neglect. Her current owner, William Rowan, bought her in 2012. At the time, *Schooner Hindu* needed restoration. With assistance from friends and family members, *Schooner Hindu* was soon ready to charter passengers again.

Year Built: 1925 • **Type of Ship:** Schooner • **Country Built:** USA • **Homeport:** Provincetown, Rhode Island • **Overall length:** 79 feet • **Beam (width at widest point):** 16 feet • **Maximum Mast Height:** 64 feet • **Armament:** She carried a .50 machine gun and depth charges during World War II • **Crew:** 1–2

Construction

Schooner Hindu has been well maintained for most of her life, with a few periods of significant restoration. She was designed by William Hand, who was also helped popularize the now-ubiquitous V-shaped powerboats. *Schooner Hindu's* distinctive style and features were inspired by the famed Grand Banks fishing schooners of old.

SS Sørlandet

St. Lawrence II: Sea Stories

The *St. Lawrence II* was built to teach young people how to sail tall ships, and the ship is dedicated to introducing young people to life aboard a traditional-style tall ship. The ship, which participates in tall ship races and extended cruises, has hosted over 20,000 teens in its lifetime, and this total attests to both her long career and the profound influence the *St. Lawrence II* has had on the sail-training world.

The *St. Lawrence II's* young crew changes with each voyage. In the winter, the ship hosts a leadership and tall ship skills program that trains students to serve as officers in charge of other students during the summer season. During the sail-training season, students have the opportunity to take turns cleaning, hoisting sails, helping with navigation and even learning how to steer the ship. The ship's programs are open to young men and women alike, and the ship sails for short voyages with periods of 'shore leave' for trainees to relax and explore each port.

The ship hosted her first group of trainees in the early 1950s, and she spends most of her time on the St. Lawrence River and on Lake Ontario. The *St. Lawrence II's* sailing program has been such a success that it served as an inspiration for the development of other sail-training organizations, including the program that operates the vessels *Playfair* and *Pathfinder* as sailing schools. Together with *St. Lawrence II*, the three ships are friendly rivals that compete in races against each other, and they frequently encounter each other at tall ship events.

Year Built: 1953; current reconstruction built in 1988 • **Type of Ship:** Brigantine • **Country Built:** Canada • **Homeport:** Kingston, Ontario, Canada • **Overall length:** 72 feet • **Beam (width at widest point):** 15 feet • **Maximum Mast Height:** 58 feet • **Armament:** None • **Crew:** 10 professional (with 23 trainees)

—————— *Construction* ——————

Like her sisters *Pathfinder* and *Playfair*, *St. Lawrence II* was designed by Francis MacLachlan for youth sail-training programs. With a hull welded from steel and a dependable diesel engine, *St. Lawrence II* is built for safety and speed. Her solid construction helps her keep up with a young crew, even as *St. Lawrence II* advances in years. Her masts have been reconstructed on several occasions; they were rebuilt in 1984 and most recently in 2014 when another reconstruction began.

Unicorn: Sea Stories

The *Unicorn* has a colorful history. Constructed in 1947, she was manufactured from materials removed from salvaged German U-boats and christened *Deo Volente I* (God Willing) and brought into service of the Dutch fishing industry. Powered by a diesel engine, she would not receive her sails until later, when she was converted to a sailing ship in 1979 after a busy fishing career. Her buyers, Peter and Agnes Kaptein of Hoorn, renamed her *Eenhoorn* (Unicorn) and decided to take her on a Mediterranean voyage. She was later sold to treasure hunter and charter ship captain Morris Henson, who sailed the *Unicorn* to the Caribbean, the Spanish Coast and other locations on charter voyages and in search of treasure. Throughout the 1980s, she sailed to distant locations around the globe and allowed her passengers to experience tall ship voyages. In the 1990s, she was purchased by Curtis and Lettie Ciszek, who sailed the *Unicorn* as a personal yacht with their family and participated in tall ship races and also continued the *Unicorn's* past career as a charter ship.

Her life took a new direction after a 1995 collision with a chemical tanker. The accident damaged the *Unicorn's* hull and prompted her owners to sell the ship. Fortunately, her new owners repaired her and returned her to sailing. She was renamed *True North* and was based out of Toronto, where she became a training ship for new sailors and tall ship skills. In 1999, she was sold once again and in 2005, she was renamed the *Unicorn* and became a sail-training vessel for a new nonprofit organization, Sisters Under Sail, that teaches young women and girls about tall ship sailing. With an all-female crew, she introduces the next generation of young women to tall ships and proudly sails the Great Lakes and abroad, often appearing at local tall ship events.

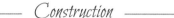

———— *Ship Details* ————

Year Built: 1947 • **Type of Ship:** Gaff-rigged topsail schooner • **Country Built:** Netherlands • **Homeport:** Asbury, New Jersey • **Overall length:** 110 feet • **Beam (width at widest point):** 19 feet • **Maximum Mast Height:** 96 feet • **Armament:** None • **Original Crew:** 5-14 (varied throughout her career) • **Present Crew:** 6

———— *Construction* ————

Much of this ship has been rebuilt and restored since her original construction. Constructed from recycled U-boats, her hull was extensively repaired following her 1995 accident. In addition to modern materials, the rebuild also incorporated spruce and Douglas fir wood. When she was registered as an American ship in 2003, she was intensively renovated and now flies the U.S. flag. Today, the *Unicorn* can accommodate ten guests and as many as six crew members for overnight voyages. She has nine passenger rooms, a captain's suite and a single room for the six crew.

Windy

Zeeto: Sea Stories

Constructed as a tribute to fishing ships of the eighteenth century, *Zeeto* bears a close resemblance to the traditional schooners that inspired her builders. Built in 1957, she has spent much of her life as a cruise ship and a yacht, and she had several different owners. She's been based on the Great Lakes since 1997, when Dave Storzok took *Zeeto* to Bayfield, where she became a cruise ship and began offering passengers the experience of tall ship sailing.

The *Zeeto* is now owned by Doug Hanson, and he jumped at the opportunity to purchase the ship when the chance came, even though he had never sailed a tall ship.

The classic-style tall ship appealed to Hanson from the beginning. As a youth, Hanson remembers seeing a tall ship enter the Duluth harbor, and this experience made a profound impact on Hanson. Once he purchased the ship, he soon sought out professional assistance to help restore *Zeeto* to her former glory. Douglas McEneany, a Duluth local and avid restorer of wooden boats, began assisting Hanson with restoring and maintaining *Zeeto*. The process occurs each winter, and new cosmetic and structural improvements are made to the *Zeeto* during the non-sailing season.

All of that hard work has paid off, and *Zeeto* graces the Great Lakes during Hanson's sailing adventures and the *Zeeto's* frequent appearances at tall ship events. One question Hanson often fields is "What's with the name?" As far as anyone can tell, the name is Greek and stands for "Long live the king"—a fitting moniker given *Zeeto's* royal appearance and character, and the royal welcome she receives from her legions of fans.

Kajama

Homeport: Toronto, Ontario, Canada

Public Programs: The *Kajama* offers a wide variety of sailing options, including daysails, dinner cruises, as well as private charters, weddings and conferences.

Available for private charters: Yes

Website: www.tallshipcruisestoronto.com

Liana's Ransom

Homeport: Halifax, Nova Scotia, Canada

Public Programs: *Liana's Ransom* hosts daysails and weekly charters, all aboard a pirate-themed vessel that actually features cannons.

Available for private charters: Yes

Website: www.lianasransom.com

Lynx

Homeport: Newmarket, New Hampshire

Public Programs: The *Lynx* offers daysails as well as a variety of educational programs, including dockside tours, history- and science-themed programs, and sailing lessons.

Available for private charters: Yes, contact the ship for more information.

Website: http://tallshiplynx.com/

Madeline

Homeport: Traverse City, Michigan

Public Programs: The *Madeline* trains students in basic and advanced sail training, and it also offers complimentary sails to nonprofits and members of the community, when possible.

Available for private charters: Contact the ship for more information.

Website: www.maritimeheritagealliance.org

Pathfinder and Playfair

Homeport: Toronto, Ontario, Canada

Public Programs: The *Pathfinder* and the *Playfair* are both operated by Toronto Brigantine, Inc., a group dedicated to teaching young people and instilling character by teaching them to operate a tall ship. Both vessels also offer daysails for adults, as well as private charters and events.

Available for private charters: Yes

Website: www.torontobrigantine.org

Pride of Baltimore II

Homeport: Baltimore, Maryland

Public Programs: The *Pride of Baltimore II* welcomes visitors aboard for deck tours, daysails, and sometimes even as guest members of the crew. It is also available for receptions, charters and other private events.

Available for private charters: Yes

Website: www.pride2.org

Red Witch

Homeport: Chicago, Illinois

Public Programs: The *Red Witch* offers a variety of public sailing options, including skyline tours, firework tours, daysails and private charters.

Available for private charters: Yes

Website: www.redwitch.com

Roseway

Homeport: Boston, Massachusetts

Public Programs: Operating in Boston and the U.S. Virgin Islands, the *Roseway* offers sail-training courses to young people, especially at-risk youth. Adults can participate on longer-term voyages and the ship can also be chartered.

Available for private charters: Yes

Website: http://worldoceanschool.org

───── S/V Denis Sullivan ─────

Homeport: Milwaukee, Wisconsin

Public Programs: The *S/V Denis Sullivan* is dedicated to educating young people about sailing, the Great Lakes, and the aquatic environment of the Great Lakes. While it's primarily a school ship, it does offer tours when participating in tall ship festivals.

Available for private charters: Yes

Website: www.schoonerdenissullivan.org

───── Schooner Hindu ─────

Homeport: Key West, Florida

Public Programs: The *Schooner Hindu* offers a number of daysails, including a Mimosa Sail, Sunset Sails, and more. It also can be rented for private events.

Available for private charters: Yes

Website: sailschoonerhindu.com

───── SS Sørlandet ─────

Homeport: Kristiansand, Norway

Public Programs: A Norwegian landmark, the *Sørlandet* operates a full-fledged high school aboard the ship, and it also participates in extended voyages that often cross entire oceans. The ship is also available for private charters.

Available for private charters: Yes

Website: www.sorlandet.org/en

───── St. Lawrence II ─────

Homeport: Kingston, Ontario, Canada

Public Programs: Dedicated to teaching youth how to sail tall ships (and the lessons they learn in the process), the *St. Lawrence II* goes on a number of week-long cruises each summer, effectively serving as a floating summer camp. While the majority of the ship's courses are geared toward young people, the ship also offers occasional classes for adults.

Available for private charters: Yes, contact the ship for more information.

Website: www.brigantine.ca

——————— Unicorn ———————

Homeport: Asbury, New Jersey

Public Programs: The *Unicorn* is unique in that it's the only all-female crewed tall ship in the world. In partnership with the nonprofit group Sisters Under Sail, it helps young women gain confidence and leadership skills aboard a tall ship.

Available for private charters: Contact the ship for more information.

Website: www.tallshipunicorn.com

——————— Windy ———————

Homeport: Chicago, Illinois

Public Programs: Located on Chicago's Navy Pier, the *Windy* offers a variety of sailing trips, from architecture tours in the Chicago harbor to "Spirit Ships and Haunted Harbors," which covers the spookier side of the region's maritime history. The *Windy* is also available for education tours, weddings, charters and other private events.

Available for private charters: Yes

Website: https://tallshipwindy.com

——————— Zeeto ———————

Homeport: Duluth, Minnesota

Public Programs: The *Zeeto* is privately owned, but it has participated in tall ship events in the past.

Available for private charters: No

Website: None

About the Author

Kaitlin Morrison is a freelance writer with a passion for interesting stories, history, and travel. Her work regularly appears in magazines and trade journals. She loves interviewing entrepreneurs, professionals and everyday people. She lives in Washington State and visits the Midwest regularly. Her visits to the Great Lakes have made a strong impression on her and provided her with inspiration while researching and writing *Tall Ships*.

Photo Credits

Appledore IV (main image) Jeff Thoreson (first inset) Joanna Poe (second inset) Cathy A. Smith (third inset) Aaron Headly (fourth inset) Cathy A. Smith (last image) Jeff Thoreson *Appledore V* (main image) BaySail, Scott Ellis (first inset) Joanna Poe (second inset) Dennis Jarvis (third inset) BaySail, Scott Ellis (fourth inset) Dennis Jarvis (last image) BaySail, Scott Ellis *Barque Europa* (main image) Kenneth Newhams, *Duluth Shipping News* (first inset) Bob Adams (second inset) Joanna Poe (third inset) Joanna Poe (fourth inset) Aaron Headly (last image) Joanna Poe *Bounty* (main image) Lyle Vincent (first inset) Shutterstock (second inset) U.S. Coast Guard, Alan Haraf (third inset) Shutterstock (fourth inset) Shutterstock (last image) Kenneth Newhams, *Duluth Shipping News Brig Niagara* (main image) Michael Greminger (first inset) Shutterstock (second inset) Shutterstock (third inset) Shutterstock (fourth inset) Shutterstock (last image) Shutterstock *Brig Roald Amundsen* (main image) Jeff Thoreson (first inset) Andrew Bone (www.flickr.com/andreboeni) (second inset) Joanna Poe (third inset) Andrew Bone (www.flickr.com/andreboeni) (fourth inset) Andrew Bone (www.flickr.com/andreboeni) (last image) Jeff Thoreson *Challenge* (main image) Great Lakes Schooner Company (first inset) Great Lakes Schooner Company (second inset) Great Lakes Schooner Company (third inset) Great Lakes Schooner Company (fourth inset) Great Lakes Schooner Company (last image) Great Lakes Schooner Company *Coaster II* (main image) Michael Greminger (first inset) Dan Downing (second inset) Dan Downing (third inset) Dan Downing (fourth inset) Dan Downing (last image) Dan Downing *Empire Sandy* (main image) Shutterstock (first inset) Boris Kasimov (second inset) Hussein Abdallah (third inset) Erin Short at Tall Ships America (fourth inset) Hussein Abdallah (last image) Scott Colbourne *Fair Jeanne* (main image) Bytown Brigantine—Tall Ships Adventure (first inset) Bytown Brigantine—Tall Ships Adventure (second inset) Bytown Brigantine—Tall Ships Adventure (third inset) Bytown Brigantine—Tall Ships Adventure (fourth inset) Shutterstock (last image) Bytown Brigantine - Tall Ships Adventure *Fazisi* (main image) *Fazizi* (first inset) *Fazizi* (second inset) *Fazizi* (third inset) *Fazizi* (fourth inset) Shutterstock (last image) *Fazizi Friends Good Will* (main image) Jeff Thoreson (first inset) Cathy A. Smith (second inset) Cathy A. Smith (third inset) U.S. Coast Guard, Senior Chief Petty Officer Tom Wunder (fourth inset) Cathy A. Smith (last image) Jeff Thoreson *Inland Seas* (main image) Dave Foster (first inset) *Inland Seas* Schoolship (second inset) *Inland Seas* Schoolship (third inset) *Inland Seas* Schoolship (fourth inset) *Inland Seas* Schoolship (last image) *Inland Seas* Schoolship *Kajama* (main image) Great Lakes Schooner Company (first inset) Great Lakes Schooner Company (second inset) Great Lakes Schooner Company (third inset) Great Lakes Schooner Company (fourth inset) Great Lakes Schooner Company (last image) Great Lakes Schooner Company *Liana's Ransom* (main image) Dennis Jarvis (first inset) Joanna Poe (second inset) Dennis Jarvis (third inset) Joanna Poe (fourth inset) Joanna Poe (last image) Alan Woodhead *Lynx* (main image) Jeff Thoreson (first inset) Cathy A. Smith (second inset) Will Scullin (third inset) Jeff Thoreson (fourth inset) Jeff Thoreson (last image) Michael Greminger *Madeline* (main image) Kathleen Maskus/Natural Solitude (first inset) Joanna Poe (second inset) Joanna Poe (third inset) Joanna Poe (fourth inset) Joanna Poe (last image) Aaron Headly *Pathfinder* (main image) Scott Proudfoot (first inset) Scott Proudfoot (second inset) Joanna Poe (third inset) Joanna Poe (fourth inset) Joanna Poe (last image) Scott Proudfoot *Playfair* (main image) Scott Proudfoot (first inset) Joanna Poe (second inset) Scott Proudfoot (third inset) Scott Proudfoot (fourth inset) Joanna Poe (last image) Joanna Poe *Pride of Baltimore II* (main image) Michael Greminger (first inset) U.S. Coast Guard, Petty Officer 3rd Class Charlotte Fritts (second inset) Amy McGovern (third inset) Joanna Poe (fourth inset) U.S. Navy photo by Mass Communication Specialist 1st Class Elisandro T. Diaz (last image) Joanna Poe *Red Witch* (main image) *Red Witch* (first inset) Jeff Thoreson (second inset) *Red Witch* (third inset) *Red Witch* (fourth inset) Shutterstock (last image) *Red Witch Roseway* (main image) Kenneth Newhams, *Duluth Shipping News* (first inset) Roseway (second inset) Shutterstock (third inset) Shutterstock (fourth inset) Roseway (last image) Kenneth Newhams, *Duluth Shipping News Denis Sullivan* (main image) Michael Greminger (first inset) Michael Greminger (second inset) Michael Greminger (third inset) Aaron Headly (fourth inset) Michael Greminger (last image) Michael Greminger *Schooner Hindu* (main image) Jeff Thoreson (first inset) Cathy A. Smith (second inset) Cathy A. Smith (third inset) Cathy A. Smith (fourth inset) Cathy A. Smith (last image) Cathy A. Smith *Sørlandet* (main image) U.S. Coast Guard photo by Auxiliarist Jonathan Roth (first inset) Jeff Thoreson (second inset) Jeff Thoreson (third inset) Jeff Thoreson (fourth inset) Jeff Thoreson (last image) Jeff Thoreson *St. Lawrence II* (main image) Martin Cathrae (first inset) Martin Cathrae (second inset) Martin Cathrae (third inset) Jesse Davis (fourth inset) Martin Cathrae (last image) Martin Cathrae *Unicorn* (main image) Jeff Thoreson (first inset) Cathy A. Smith (second inset) Joanna Poe (third inset) Jeff Thoreson (fourth inset) Joanna Poe (last image) Jeff Thoreson *Windy* (main image) *Windy*, Lynn Randall (first inset) Shutterstock (second inset) Shutterstock (third inset) Shutterstock (fourth inset) Shutterstock (last image) Shutterstock *Zeeto* (main image) Kenneth Newhams, *Duluth Shipping News* (first inset) Lois Bravo (second inset) Lois Bravo (third inset) Lois Bravo (fourth inset) Lois Bravo (last image) Lois Bravo